D

10,214

REACHING FOR THE STARS

ROSEANNE

TV's Funny Lady

by Bob Italia

Published by Abdo & Daughters, 6535 Cecilia Circle, Edina, Minnesota 55439.

Library bound edition distributed by Rockbottom Books, Pentagon Tower, P.O. Box 36036, Minneapolis, MN 55435.

Library of Congress Number: 91-073035   ISBN: 1-56239-058-9

Cover photo: Retna Ltd.
Inside photos: Pictorial Parade: 4, 16, 27, 29, 31; Retna Ltd.: 8, 10, 18, 25; FPG International: 23

Edited by Rosemary Wallner

TABLE OF CONTENTS

4

AMERICA'S FUNNIEST HOUSEWIFE

She has been called brash, crude, rotund—and very funny. Her television show is one of America's most popular. Her fans say she speaks for America.

I figure when my husband comes home at night, if the kids are still alive, then I've done my job.

She is a simple woman. She has an ordinary appearance. Yet when she speaks, her whiny voice sets her apart from everyone else.

I love my husband and I love my kids, but I need something more—like maybe a life!

She is similar to her famous television character. She's clever, outspoken, and a real smartmouth.

My husband asks, Do we have any Chee-tos left— like he couldn't lift up the sofa cushions himself?

She's America's funniest housewife. She's Roseanne Barr Arnold.

In the 1980s, Roseanne Barr became America's funniest housewife.

GROWING UP
IN UTAH

Roseanne Barr was born on November 3, 1952, in Salt Lake City, Utah. Her mother, Helen, was a cashier at a fast-food restaurant. Her father, Jerry, had a heart condition and could not hold a steady job. He worked at a department store, then as a door-to-door salesman of jewelry and blankets. Barr had a younger brother, Ben, and two younger sisters, Geraldine and Stephanie.

Barr lived with her family in an apartment that her grandparents owned. The Barrs did not have a lot of money. "My father wore the same outfit for about two weeks," Barr recalled. "About every two weeks, he'd call us kids together and say, 'Kids, go draw me a bath.' We'd cheer and run around, kiss our mother, clean our rooms."

When Barr was four years old, her mother joined the Mormon Church. By the time she was eight years old, Barr was speaking at the local Mormon church. "I would always give the speeches for the youth," she said.

Barr was president of the church's Youth Group, and she also led the choir. Barr thought she would one day become a mother, teacher, or secretary.

Barr spent a lot of time with her grandmother, Bobbe Mary. "I loved my grandmother more than any other human being," said Barr, "because she never lied, never told you what you wanted to hear, never compromised."

Barr used to go to Bobbe's apartment in Salt Lake City almost every day. There she would play cards with her grandmother, snoop in her closets, play in the junked cars Bobbe had in her backyard—and eat. When Barr wasn't at her grandmother's, she was at home doing chores and practicing the piano.

When she was older, Barr and her family moved into their own house. Barr had her own room—in the attic.

Barr learned about comedy from her father. They would take turns making fun of each other. "My father taught me that comedy is mightier than the sword and the pen," she said. "We would go around and around and he would say things about women and I would say things about him and we would have contests and showdowns and I would always win."

Roseanne Barr's interest in comedy began when she was a young girl growing up in Salt Lake City, Utah.

When a comedian would appear on the "Ed Sullivan Show," her father would call out: "Comedian! Comedian!" Then everyone in the house would run in and sit down to watch the television. Said Barr, " 'Comedy,' he told me, 'is funniest when it's about speaking up for the little man.' " Barr's father had always wanted to be a stand-up comic, but he never got the chance.

LEARNING TO ENTERTAIN

Barr also learned to be an entertainer at a very young age. She and a friend, Sherri, put on a neighborhood play every summer. "I would spend a few days writing it," Barr explained, "and it always had music, we would sing the popular songs of the day with a few word changes. We would force all of our friends and our little sisters into playing the foils." They made costumes out of construction paper. They even printed tickets and invitations.

"Mostly it would just be our parents and siblings who came," said Barr. "They would applaud nicely. My mom and dad would always go out of their way for me and my plays. I could always be assured of their standing ovation for all my efforts."

Barr was known to be a bossy child. "I always insisted on being the teacher when we played school," she said, "the mother when we played house, and the star of every neighborhood play. I didn't feel then that hogging all the glory is a disservice. I can do it better than anyone."

She could also be very strange. "I'd do really weird things as a kid," Barr said, "like walk down the middle of a highway with blankets over my head. I was always trying to do things in Utah that would shock people because it was the most boring place on earth.

"My parents always thought I was really amusing," she added. "But they also thought I was dangerous. They would tell me not to do something, but then they would laugh when I did it."

"I'd do really weird things as a kid," Roseanne Barr has admitted. Today, she's known and loved for all the weird things she jokes about.

Barr's schoolmates remember her as someone who entertained everyone—including teachers—with funny stories and a sharp tongue. "Everyone knew Barr in school because she was so funny," said one of Barr's childhood friends.

THE ACCIDENT

When Barr was a sophomore at East High School, she was hit by a car when she tried to cross a street near her home. She received a severe concussion in the accident. "I like died, or whatever you call it," said Barr. "When I woke up, I wasn't the same person, because I had gone to a place where I guess a lot of people don't go, and when I came back, it was all going to be *my* way."

Barr wasn't the same after the accident. "Her grades dropped," recalled a former classmate. "She didn't seem to care about anything anymore. She took her father's car joy-riding one night before she got her license. She cracked [the car] up, and her dad was furious."

"After the accident," Barr recalled, "I had a lot of trouble focusing and remembering things. I had always been an 'A' student, and now suddenly, the concept of math began to fade and I couldn't understand it anymore.

"I was afraid to sleep, and sometimes I would make it for days without it. Once, I hadn't slept for several days, and was sitting in my mother's living room where my eyes rolled back and I went into convulsions. I think this is when Mama started to think about having me hospitalized."

A year later, Barr had a mental breakdown at a Mormon meeting. "Rosie started shouting," a friend remembered. "She said, 'You're all hypocrites, all hypocrites!' " Soon after, seventeen-year-old Barr was placed in the Utah state hospital. She stayed there for almost a year.

In the hospital, Barr was given drugs that helped her sleep. Her head injury healed, and she got better. But the year in the hospital was not pleasant.

"It was a horrifying place," said Barr, "and I was very heavily drugged, so I saw everything through a pretty intense fog. It was a place where you come out of and you become something else, or else you die. I came out."

LEAVING HOME

After she left the hospital, Barr, now nineteen years old, took a trip to Georgetown, Colorado, to visit a childhood friend, Linda Rizzardi. There she met Bill Pentland, a motel clerk. She fell in love with him.

"I was real lucky the day I met Bill," Barr said. "He's the coolest person I've ever met. Nobody is funnier or smarter or nicer."

When she was in Colorado, Barr got a job as an assistant chef at the Silver Queen, a French restaurant. She often got into fights with the head chef. Eventually, Barr was demoted to dishwasher. Shortly after, she resigned.

Barr and Bill Pentland were married two years later. They had three children, Jessica, Jennifer, and Jacob. In 1980, they moved to Denver, Colorado, and bought a house. Barr stayed at home and Bill worked, first as a garbageman, then as a postal worker.

Barr was getting bored as a housewife. She wanted to become a poet or a writer. She eventually found a part-time job as a window dresser in a clothing store, then began thinking about becoming a buyer in the clothing industry.

Barr also was involved in the women's rights movement. She spent a lot of time at the Women To Women Bookstore in Denver, reading books on women's rights.

BECOMING A COMEDIAN

Because she wasn't making enough money as a window dresser, Barr became a cocktail waitress for a popular restaurant in 1981. There, Barr developed a quick wit to deal with all the wise-cracking male customers.

"I really felt like a star," she said. "I was receiving all the male attention. I very much enjoyed it, and my customers used to come in every day. I owe these men so much, because it was because of them that I knew there was a place for me in comedy."

As a result of her hard work at comedy clubs, Roseanne Barr won an award at the 1988 American Comedy Awards.

One of the patrons suggested that Barr go to the Comedy Shoppe in Denver where comedians could get up on stage and tell jokes.

"I started to think about it," she said. "For a year it was in my head and I was even writing my material. When I finally went, several of my customers went down there with me and cheered me on. I went on stage and did my show and people just loved it."

Barr worked her comedy routine every Monday at Straite Johnson's for four months. She tape-recorded her routines and listened to them to see where she could improve.

The owner of the Three Sisters nightclub heard Barr's routine and hired her as a regular comedian. While she was at the Three Sisters, Barr thought up the idea for a routine she called "The Domestic Goddess."

"When I started doing that act," she said, "suddenly I was just so popular. I headlined my very first time out in Kansas City with twenty minutes of an act and twenty minutes of playing around and made $500 for the week. It was the best show I ever had in my life. I had a standing ovation every night. That was when I started getting good.

"The domestic goddess routine came about when I was a little girl of about nine or ten," she added. "

My mother and all the neighbor ladies were reading a book called *Fascinating Womanhood*. One of the chapters in the book explained how to be a domestic goddess by turning yourself into [an obedient] wife. That book really scared me because I thought that's what growing up and being a woman was all about. It's so funny and tragic what was put on women and girls in the [1950s]."

Barr continued to practice and polish her act. Then she entered the Denver Laugh-Off contest. There were seventeen contestants entered in the four-night event. Barr was the only woman. When she won, Barr thought it was time to try to make the big time in Los Angeles. Even comic Louie Anderson encouraged Barr to go to Los Angeles.

Barr went to the Comedy Store in Los Angeles and auditioned for Mitzi Shore. Shore was responsible for launching the careers of Richard Pryor, David Letterman, Robin Williams, and many other famous comedians. If she could impress Shore, Barr would become a star.

One of Roseanne Barr's earliest comedy routines was titled "The Domestic Goddess."
Fans loved her jokes about housework, grocery shopping, and families.

"The night I auditioned for Mitzi Shore," Barr remembered, "I went on stage for six minutes and blew the room away. It was the greatest five-minute set I ever had. As I went off stage, Mitzi Shore said, 'Go do twenty minutes in the Main Room.' All the waitresses said she had never done that before, took someone from Show Case to Main Room in the same night. After my twenty minutes Mitzi said, 'You gotta move out to LA, Roseann-A, I'll take care of you. You are going to be one who breaks down the doors of comedy for women.'"

Barr went to Los Angeles to rehearse an act that Shore was producing for television. Shore took her shopping for an appropriate stage costume.

"I ended up wearing a pair of funky designer cotton overalls," Barr said, "because as Mitzi pointed out to me, 'You should always wear overalls because yours is a kind of farm act anyway.'"

ROSEANNE BARR'S BIG BREAK

After a dress rehearsal of her television act, Barr was approached by Jim McCowley, the talent coordinator for "The Tonight Show." "I'm putting you on the show," McCowley said to Barr. "Can you come to my office tomorrow?" Barr said yes.

Afterwards, Barr met her sister Geraldine in the parking lot and they danced, cried, and celebrated for forty-five minutes. Then they went inside and called Bill and their parents to tell them the good news.

The next day, Barr met with Jim McCowley in the Burbank, California office of "The Tonight Show." McCowley listened to Barr's act and told her which parts she could perform on television. The very next night, Barr appeared on "The Tonight Show." She was an instant hit.

"The best part of getting on 'The Tonight Show,'" said Barr, "was that I was able to go directly from the clubs in Denver to a concert tour. I never had to really work clubs. They would have killed me. I would've never made it."

After her appearance on "The Tonight Show," Barr's career took off. She toured with singer Julio Iglesias for four months, appeared on "Late Night With David Letterman," then returned to "The Tonight Show" as a performer *and* a guest. She even taped a special comedy show on cable TV's HBO (Home Box Office) channel.

A TELEVISION SHOW AND A MOVIE

In 1986, Barr's husband and children moved from Denver to Hollywood. Producers approached Barr with television and movie deals. The television show came first.

"I told my agent I didn't want to be on the road anymore," said Barr. "It took many meetings with many producers."

"Roseanne" debuted in October 1988 on the ABC Television Network. The show features Roseanne Barr as a wise-cracking mother who works in a plastics factory, and her equally funny blue-collar husband, played by John Goodman.

Roseanne Barr and her TV-husband John Goodman practice a scene for the ABC-TV series "Roseanne."

All of America fell in love with Barr's sharp wit and down-to-earth humor. Eventually, "Roseanne" unseated the NBC-TV sitcom "The Cosby Show" as America's most popular television show.

"My character is just like a mom," said Barr. "She doesn't clean her house. She isn't sweet all the time. And she doesn't pay attention to her kids and husband."

But the success of "Roseanne" did not come easily. Barr was used to simple comedy routines with quick one-liners. For the television show, she had to memorize a script—and often forgot her lines.

Barr also had problems working with a crew. In all her years as a comic, she had worked alone. Now other actors, directors, and producers were involved. Barr got into many arguments and often stormed off the set.

Eventually Barr saw the foolishness of her actions. She was earning $30,000 a week plus fifteen percent of the money paid by advertisers. She decided not to overreact and to become more professional. She took acting lessons, and listened to advice from costar John Goodman. Her new attitude helped make "Roseanne" a huge success.

The cast of "Roseanne" includes Sara Gilbert (left), Roseanne Barr, John Goodman, and Lecy Goranson.

In 1989, Barr made her first movie, *She-Devil,* where she starred with Meryl Streep. Again she had many difficulties. She was used to acting on television. Acting in a movie was very different.

"Roseanne seems so sure of herself," said a fellow actress, "but she's confident only in areas where she's had experience or success—like delivering one-liners. Beyond that, she's insecure, and that makes her defensive."

Barr argued with Streep and director Susan Seidelman about the dialogue and acting techniques. But eventually, Barr saw that she should take the advice of those around her. *She-Devil* was completed and became a moderate success at the box office.

After *She-Devil,* Barr's fifteen-year marriage to Bill Pentland began failing. Barr had met Tom Arnold, a comedian, during the filming of the movie. In 1990, Barr divorced Pentland and married Arnold.

"Things were pretty difficult at home," she said. "I was working sixteen hours a day. I wasn't there. Even when I was there, I wasn't there. We had to admit that things were real bad and weren't going to get any better."

In 1990, Roseanne Barr married her second husband, comedian Tom Arnold.

These days, Roseanne Arnold must battle with her tremendous success—and stories about her weight (she is five-foot-four-inches and weighs over 200 pounds).

"I was thin once," she said. "I got really scared because I got too skinny. So I went all the way the other way. I think women should try to increase their size rather than decrease it. I believe the bigger we are, the more space we'll take up and the more we'll have to be reckoned with."

Roseanne and husband Tom Arnold enjoy their careers–and enjoy making their fans laugh.

THE SECRET
OF HER SUCCESS

Why is Roseanne so popular? She is a down-to-earth woman with whom many feel at ease. She is a real person—and she makes people laugh. Says Mitzi Shore: "I think that Roseanne really represents America."

And what does Roseanne think of her success? "I feel the same way as I did when I left Salt Lake City," she said. "The only difference is that now I can buy more."

Down-to-earth, and funny. That's Roseanne Barr Arnold.

In 1990, Roseanne gained further recognition as a comedian when she won a People's Choice Award.

ROSEANNE'S ADDRESS

You can write to Roseanne Arnold at:

Roseanne Arnold
c/o "Roseanne"
ABC-TV
2040 Avenue of the Stars
Los Angeles, CA 90067

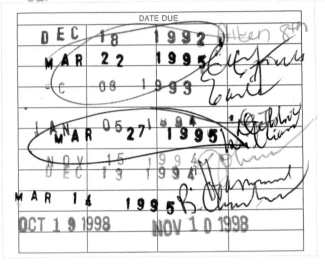

921
Ba

Italia, Robert, 1955

Roseanne Barr

10,314 $10.95